"They'll Outgrow It..."

And Other Myths

The Best of Cartoons for Parents

Selected and Written
by Leah Yarrow

WOODBINE HOUSE • 1986

Published in the United States by Woodbine House, Inc

Library of Congress Catalogue Card Number: 86-050458
ISBN: 0-933149-07-7
Cover Design: Carol Schwartz
Book Design: Michael Walsh
Typesetting: Wordscape, Washington, D.C.
Manufactured in the United States of America

1 2 3 4 5 6 7 8 9 10

Acknowledgments

The task of locating the many cartoonists represented in this volume proved to be much greater than I had ever imagined. It would have been impossible without the help of the following people, to whom I am deeply grateful:

Ruth Rogin, of the Cartoonists Association, who gave unsparingly of her time and expertise;

Doris Cohen and Sylvia Roth, of Rothco Cartoons, Inc., who in a very short time helped identify and locate cartoonists who they do not represent as well as those they do, and searched their files for cartoons appropriate for this collection;

Lee Lorenz, art director of *The New Yorker*;

Marge Divine, of the National Cartoonists Society;

Chuck Green, of the Museum of Cartoon Art; and

the many librarians at the following libraries: Evanston, Wilmette, Skokie, Lincolnwood, and Chicago, Illinois; Abington, Pennsylvania; and the research librarians at *The New Yorker*.

For each cartoon in this book, the publisher and I have been scrupulous in contacting the owners of copyright and in obtaining permission to reprint. If we have unwittingly overlooked any interest, necessary apologies and acknowledgements will be made.

I would like to thank my editor, Marshall Levin, for his unflagging support and enthusiasm for this project, his care in preserving the integrity of the volume's concept, and his insightful editing.

I'd also like to extend my thanks and congratulations to all the cartoonists whose work appears in these pages. Their ability to capture the essence of parenting and children is remarkable.

Last, but not least, I want to thank my husband and my children for their support and encouragement and for providing the comic relief that was the seed from which this book grew.

Leah Yarrow
October 1986

Contents

Introduction

Parents today take "parenting" more seriously than ever before. A glance along the crowded shelves of the child care section in most bookstores is proof that parenting is a popular topic.

But the glut of guidance, from prenatal care to adolescence, has created a sense of confusion among parents who are doing so much research for this lifetime job. The pendulum, said to swing back with every generation, is instead spinning. Our parents had Spock as their baby book bible. One voice told them how to parent. Not today. Goodbye, Spock—Hello, Brazelton, White, Leach, Bronfenbrenner, Caplan, Fraiberg, and others. For every author who says not to let your baby cry, there's one to argue the opposite, and one to say let him cry sometimes. Parents debate the child-rearing philosophies of their favorite authors with the same ferocity they once debated politics.

And underneath it all is this terrible uneasiness—Am I doing the right thing? Will Johnny (or these days more likely Jason or Joshua) be scarred for life because he wasn't introduced to *Goodnight Moon* until he was three, or because he kept his pacifier until he was eight? This is what is keeping parents up at night. (Their children, of course, are sleeping deeply—albeit perhaps in the family bed.) It's enough to make a parent nuts.

What's missing from today's parenting is a sense of humor about it all. I know, because I've spent more than my share of sleepless nights over having mentioned the word "potty" before my daughter was "ready." And I've built up enough phone message units to land us in the poor house by talking to friends about whether I discipline my children too little—or too much. (Why should I think I'm doing it right?) Picture me and my husband, holding hands and clenching our teeth, tears in our eyes, while we sat listening to our eight-month-old son scream when we decided that we couldn't get up every half hour through the night. I thought I was going to be sick.

But if I could have stepped away and had a bird's eye view of the situation, I think I would have laughed—or at least chuckled. If only I had known then that other parents went to the same ridiculous lengths, that they felt those same turbulent emotions and fears.

I remember one night reading a copy of Lynn Johnston's *No More Washtub Blues* in bed with my husband. We laughed so hard the tears ran. We recognized ourselves, we recognized our friends and our children, and we recognized the hilarity, the loveliness, the universality of parenting. When my son cried out that night I felt different when I went to him. I was less anxious, more relaxed. I had a new perspective. The laughter had been healing.

In this book I hope to give you those same gifts—the exquisite relief that comes from knowing you are not alone with your fears, exasperations, vascillations, quandaries, and (let's not forget) joys.

These cartoons celebrate the best and the worst about raising children. You will see that some ideas have changed. Thirty years ago many cartoons poked fun at fathers pacing the waiting room floor while their wives were in the delivery room. You won't find cartoons like that now. Social change has given us new situations to laugh at—and Gary Trudeau, for example, does a splendid job of skewering the new fatherhood. In a couple of frames we grasp the essence of the conflict today's fathers feel as they attempt to take an active role in parenting and the frustration today's mothers feel because their great expectations for their husband's involvement often remain unmet. Cartoons twenty years ago captured the plight of the homemaker and housewife. Today's cartoons deal with working mothers, the supermom syndrome, delayed childbearing, and other current issues.

But these cartoons also depict the timeless aspects of parenting. Our parents and our parents' parents before them clung to each other in the middle of the night when the baby cried for the fourth time or when their daughter left for her first date. Since the beginning of time, children have had to go to the bathroom *after* they were dressed in shirt, overalls, sweater, snowpants, snowjacket, boots, hat, and mittens.

So put your kids to bed and your feet up. Let yourself relax and laugh. I know you'll feel better. I did.

Becoming a Parent 1

In a *Parents Magazine* poll many years ago I asked mothers to tell us when they started to feel like parents. Some said they felt like a parent during pregnancy. But a good number—about 25 percent—only began to feel like a parent from two months to a year or more after giving birth. That each of us feels parentlike at different stages is an interesting comment on the process of becoming a parent.

I truly believe that, just as there are predictable and obvious signs of pregnancy, there are signs of blossoming parenthood as well. These are mostly intangible cues that separate parents from the nonparents of the world. But just as fellow countrymen seem instinctively to recognize one another, so can we usually identify the parents among us. Maybe it's the reassuring smile I'll give the lady in front of me at the supermarket who has an overflowing cart of groceries and a three year old screaming for a package of gum. I know I can often be spotted because of the stickers slapped on my back, shoulders, or knees by my children when I'm not looking. These are badges of parenthood to outsiders.

"Parent" is also written all over my pocketbook. When I reach inside for a pen to write a check, chances are I'll grab a crayon instead. The contents of my purse, often spilled on the floor of a store, is a dead giveaway. It's a treasure trove for kids. In addition to crayons and markers, there are coloring books and plain paper, a deck of cards, balloons, an empty needless syringe from my son's last allergy shot, cracker crumbs, and dozens of pieces of chewed gum wrapped in paper or tissue. Mom is always the nearest garbage can.

And of course there are the discarded stickers I've pulled off of my clothes when someone has said, "Excuse me, do you know you have a Garbage Pail Kid's sticker stuck to your back?" If I weren't a parent, would I be carrying those things around?

But these are physical signs of parenthood—like fatigue, like always rocking when you're standing as if you've got a baby in your arms, like the fact that one hip will always be slightly higher than the other because you've carried your children around so much.

However, when I asked when the mothers in that *Parents* poll began to feel like parents, I meant something different. I was asking about the psychological and emotional grip that parenthood holds on you, whether you're a mom or dad. It is an identity like no other; we wear it throughout our lives like a second skin. We may change careers, philosophies, religions, marriage partners. You could even have a sex change operation and your identity as "parent" would cling to the alterations.

What are these psychological and emotional changes I'm talking about? I'll tell you, though they are probably already familiar to you.

I first noticed how my thinking had changed when I realized that parenthood colored my notion of what going out and having a good time was all about. Parenthood means I measure everything in terms of convenience and tolerance of children. Is the grocery store "stroller-accessible?" Does the restaurant have high chairs or booster seats? Can you get hot dogs as well as steak au poivre? Restaurants that serve breadsticks while you peruse the menu earn my highest praise. A subway or bus trip becomes an outing in itself, not a means to an end. Through the eyes of a parent every venture is analyzed according to a new math equation: entertainment value divided by aggravation level equals destination. A walk, for instance, rates high on the entertainment value side of the equation. But when you figure in the aggravation components you may stay home. (Will he sit in the stroller or insist on walking, especially in the opposite direction from whichever way you're going? If it's hot will he insist on a coat? If it's cold will she argue for the sleeveless dress? Will they try to pull away from you as you're crossing the street? Will they nag for a cookie from the bakery or a banana from the fruit market or a ride on the merry-go-round in front of the five-and-dime? And what about that riding toy he promised he would ride *all* the way?) If you do go out, at least you know what to expect, right?

I knew I'd become a parent when I discovered a deep conflict between the values I set for myself and those I wanted to establish for my child. This comes under the title of setting an example and why it's so hard. Very early on I, like many other parents, decided my children would be raised in as sugar-free an environment as possible. No cookies, no cake. And lollipops—banish the thought! I, however, was raised in an era when sugar was allowed: frosted flakes, Hostess cupcakes, all the good stuff. Sure, I eat healthy foods, but I also need my quota of junk. This was not a problem when the kids were babies. You eat in front of them, they don't know what it is. They're happy if you give them a bagel to chew on. A few months down the line, though, when they figure out you have something good, you have to become more cunning. I learned to wait until naptime. When they stopped taking naps, I sneaked a bite of donut during Sesame Street.

I didn't feel good about it, mind you. But it was a craving, and I was so glad it was one my children didn't have. Finally it got to the point where I had to forgo sweets during the day altogether. By evening I could barely stand it. As soon as the kids were in bed, into the kitchen I went. Unfortunately, my son's bedroom used to be on the hallway that joins the kitchen to the living room. Thinking that he was fast asleep, I would dish myself some ice cream and tiptoe back down the hall for a favorite TV program. Just as I slipped past his door I would hear a little voice. "Watcha got there, Mom?" Caught. Twinges of guilt and remorse. "Nothing, honey, just going to watch some TV," I'd mumble. "Moooooom," he would say, exasperated. "I know you always have treats in front of TV. What are you *having?*"

And from my daughter came this: My husband read the kids their bedtime stories while I, unable to control my sweet attack, sneaked a treat in the kitchen. When it came time to say goodnight, I slipped into my daughter's room, leaned over and kissed her goodnight. "Mmm, Mommy, your breath smells good. Is that chocolate?" Caught in a stranglehold of righteous values, I vowed to give up sweets forever (until they're definitely asleep).

Another example of these value conflicts happened when my son was turning two and my parents came to visit for his birthday. Out for a walk, Benjamin stubbed his toe on the sidewalk. "Oh sh-t!" he shrieked with a wild grin. My parents looked at me. "He said 'I slipped,'" I told them. His language was quite lispy and mushy at that point and I figured I could get away with it. But as the day continued, Benjy said "Oh sh-t" so many times that I could no longer deny it. Luckily my parents thought it was hilarious. Again, the conflict between what was right for me and for the kids had to be cleared up. Now my language is much less polluted than it was before I became a parent.

Priorities change, too, as we become parents in earnest. Family time is more important than career, perhaps, sleep more important than the late, late movie. The most meaningful people in your life once you're a parent are your pediatrician, your family, the all-night pharmacist, friends with children, and everyone else (in that order). This is not necessarily something we like, or even choose. It's just a fact of life.

Becoming a parent also teaches you flexibility and the art of compromise. When my children were babies they had no schedules. I never knew when they were going to eat, when they would sleep. At first I found it incredibly frustrating. How could I ever get anything done? I've always been a fairly organized person. It took babies to show me the freedom of flexibility, the practicality of using time when you have it, whenever that might be. If you see people who make good use of their time, chances are they're parents.

Compromise and patience are two other skills parenthood has taught me. I learned to play two games of bingo at 6:30 A.M. so I could have one almost-uninterrupted conversation an hour later. I learned not to fall apart when the pretzel I packed for a child's snack came out slightly broken and the kid had an attack. (I *know* I'm not the only one to scotch tape food back together.) The experience we parents all have had soothing ruffled feathers, making treaties between warring siblings, creating livable laws, arbitrating, and getting at the underlying meaning of a problem qualifies each of us to be career diplomats. Too bad we don't have time for outside pursuits.

Our world view changes, too, as parents. You realize that even soldiers are someone else's children. Pollution means our children can't breathe, or swim in the lake like we once did. We have an investment in the future that people without children do not have. The issues of safety (speed limits, traffic lights, stop signs, well-lit streets, abduction), education, conservation, government–these become personal. We may not act on all of them, but they have new and deeper meaning for us.

Among the many other ways that parenthood molds us there is one last characteristic that I want to mention. It's a protective mechanism that seems to develop early on. I call it "amnesia for the bad times." Both of my children (but I hope not this third one waiting to be born) had terrible colic for months after birth. They screamed, kicked, had gas, had trouble nursing, et cetera. I can tell you all this because it's in the kids' baby books and because it's not something I can forget completely.

But what I don't remember is how bad it felt, emotionally. I can close my eyes and remember every detail of how Benjy looked and how I felt when he first began to smile. I remember every detail and how I felt when he discovered sunbeams on the floor. I can still see Aliza scooting backwards until half her body was under the couch before she learned to crawl. All my senses have memories of the joy of the children at every age. I can smell them as babies. But only my brain can tell me about the troubles: the endless weeks of illness, tantrums, the various stages that we tried to cope with (terrible ones, twos, threes, fours, fives, ad infinitum).

When I became pregnant this time, many people congratulated us and in the same breath said, "Well, hope you get a lot of sleep now!"
Now, after two children who never slept, we of all people should not need to be reminded. Sure, I remember that I'll be tired. But my amnesia for the bad times reminds me that those things are temporary, while the magic and challenge of having children remain. And that's how, and why, we become parents.

cathy®
by Cathy Guisewite
AND SO I...
LOOK, HONEY! HE'S BURPING UP!
DOES OUR POOKIE NEED A WIDDLE WIPEY?
DADDY-WADDY WUBS THE TUMMY!
MOMMY-WOMMY WUVS YOU!
THIS IS MAKING ME SICK. COME ON, CATHY.
MAX DIDN'T MEAN IT. WE LOVE YOUR LITTLE BABY.
IT'S YOU WE CAN'T STAND ANYMORE.
© 1985 Universal Press Syndicate
6·5 Guisewite
SYVERSON

"You hate my guts, don't you?"

"It's better than using force!"

"Having a baby really puts a cat in perspective."

cathy®
by Cathy Guisewite
IT'S TYPICAL FOR WOMEN WHO HAVE BEEN REAL GO-GETTERS IN BUSINESS TO TURN THAT SAME PASSION ONTO THE EXPERIENCE OF PARENTING.
SOME START WITH FLASH CARDS AND MUSIC LESSONS WHEN THEIR BABY IS JUST A WEEK OLD. YOU'RE NOT GOING TO DO THAT ARE YOU, ANDREA?
START EDUCATING THE BABY A WEEK AFTER BIRTH ?? DON'T BE RIDICULOUS.
WE WOULD HAVE MISSED THE WHOLE NINE MONTHS OF PREGNANCY!
..THIS NEXT SELECTION IS FROM VIVALDI, LITTLE ONE...
© 1986 Universal Press Syndicate
2-4
Guisewite

J. Whiting

Reprinted by permission: Tribune Media Services

Feb. 1982 Good Housekeeping. Reprinted by permission of Orlando Busino.

"Oh, all right, all right! I'll UNzip it so that you can ZIP it!"

For Better or For Worse®

by Lynn Johnston

For Better or For Worse® **by Lynn Johnston**

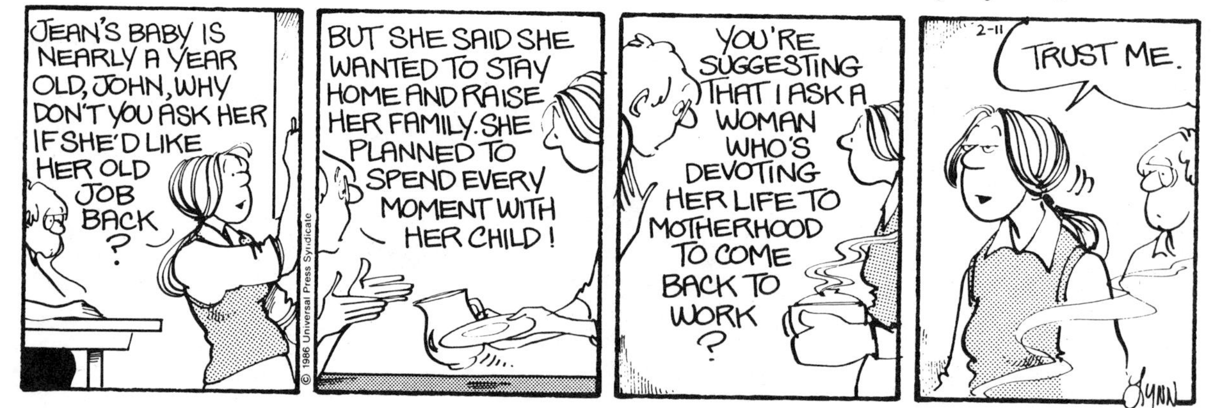

For Better or For Worse®
by Lynn Johnston
I'VE GOT 3 MONTHS LEFT TO GO, EL... AND ALREADY I'M SO SICK OF MATERNITY CLOTHES.
...SAME OLD THING DAY IN, DAY OUT...
BUT I THOUGHT YOU SAID YOU HAD AN OUTFIT FOR EVERY DAY OF THE WEEK!
I DO.
THIS IS IT!
4-2
© 1986 Universal Press Syndicate
LYNN

cathy®
by Cathy Guisewite
BONNE NUIT, MON BÉBÉ!
NOW YOU'RE SPEAKING FRENCH TO YOUR UNBORN CHILD THROUGH A PAPER TOWEL TUBE??
IT'S PROVEN THAT A BABY CAN LEARN TO RECOGNIZE VOICES AND SIMPLE WORDS BEFORE BIRTH, CATHY...
...SO WHY NOT INTRODUCE THE CONCEPT OF FOREIGN LANGUAGE?
BUONA NOTTE, BAMBINO.
IT KICKED!!
TRI-LINGUAL!!
SHEESH.
OY VAY.
© 1986 Universal Press Syndicate
GUISEWITE 4-1

"How's everything, otherwise?"

cathy®

by Cathy Guisewite

HAVE YOU PAINTED THE BABY'S ROOM YET, ANDREA ?

NO, BUT WE HAVE BOUGHT BABY'S FIRST ISOKINETIC WORKOUT WAGON... AN ERGONOMIC STROLLER... COMPACT DISC MUSICAL MOBILE... A PC WITH INTERACTIVE, PRE-VERBAL SOFTWARE... A "BUSY BOX" WITH 32-DIGIT AUTO-REDIAL...

CRIB SHEETS PRINTED WITH THE WORKS OF THE 17TH-CENTURY MASTERS.... FLASH CARDS... ENOUGH LEGO SETS TO RECONSTRUCT MANHATTAN... NON-TOXIC MARKERS COLOR COORDINATED WITH BABY'S HAND-LOOMED VCR COVER... AND A STUFFED LEMUR THAT PLAYS THE OPERAS OF PUCCINI!!

HAVE YOU PAINTED THE BABY'S CONDOMINIUM YET ?

GUISEWITE 4-4

For Better or For Worse®

by Lynn Johnston

"You have a healthy, eight-pound baby boy, Mrs. McKeever. . . . Get up!"

"Wait, let me remember you just the way you are."

"WELL, HE STARTED IT!"

"Your Honor, this woman gave birth to a naked child!"

"I feel like God!"

The World As They See It 2

How often, in a department or grocery store, have you felt little fingers clench the material covering your knees? Looking down you see a pint-sized being, holding on for dear life to the limb he believes belongs to his mother or father. "I'm sorry, honey, you've got the wrong knee," I say. The innocent face turns up toward my voice and, just as the shock wears off and the child begins to wail, the real mom or dad comes to claim him. The world, as they see it, is a collection of many-colored knees.

- When we lived in New York and my son Benjy was about two years old, the order of our days was dictated by the alternate-side-of-the-street parking regulations. We rarely took the car to do anything, except to move it from one side of the street to the other. Little did we realize the impact this almost daily ritual had on Benjy until one night at bedtime when he asked his dad about the sun. Dad explained, with his limited knowledge of astronomy, how the sun was on our side of the world part of the day and on the other side of the world the other part of the day. When he finished his explanation, Benjy asked with a look of concern on his face, "Do you think the sun will find a parking space?" In the world as they see it, even celestial bodies have human concerns.
- Just as Benjamin turned three, we signed him up for preschool. We explained that preschool was a place for him to play with other children and toys, to learn new things, do crafts, sing songs, and more. He seemed pleased with the idea. Like many parents, I decided it would be easier if I didn't have to drive twice a day, every day, so I arranged to share the driving with another mother who lived nearby. One day, before school began, I was telling Benjamin that we had arranged for a carpool to school. Suddenly, the child who had been so eager to scamper out the front door became a weeping mess. "I won't go!" he screamed over and over. I tried to reason

with him, but with no success. Finally I got the brilliant idea to ask him why he was so against the carpool idea. "I don't know how to swim!" he wailed. The world, as they see it, can have cars filled with water and uncaring parents who don't even think to send a life preserver.

- Aliza, our four-year-old daughter, was working on a coloring project with several other children at the local library when one of the little girls said to her, in a voice dripping with snobbery, "You're just doing scribble-scrabble!" "I am not!" Aliza retorted. "You are too, it's just scribble-scrabble," the girl repeated with even greater contempt. Aliza continued to argue, her face growing redder, her voice quieter and shakier, until I couldn't stand it any longer. I stepped in, gave the girl a piece of my mind, and left them to finish their projects. A short time later I came to collect Aliza to go home. "Mom," she said, "can Ashley (the girl who made fun of her artwork) come over to our house and play?" Shocked (no, appalled) I barked out, "No, not today," and threw my most wicked look at this little Ashley. All the way home, Aliza expressed bewilderment at my unfriendly response. "Why?" she asked. "Why can't she come over?" In the world as they see it, enemies turn into friends just as frogs turn into princes.
- In the middle of Benjy's third month of first grade, his teacher got the flu and was absent from school for a few days. I tried to find out something about the substitute from him. "What was she like?" I asked. "Okay," he said in his usual verbose and informative style. "Well, was she young or old?" I asked. "I don't know," he said. "Kinda old, I guess." "Did she look the same age as Miss B.?" I asked again. Miss B. is in her late twenties. "I think so," he said. "Yes, I guess she was old." In the world as they see it, all adults are about the same age—old!
- When I was a small child living on the south side of Chicago, my parents once told me as a joke that we owned a yacht in a harbor that we often drove by. Little did they realize what fantasy that joke

launched. I daydreamed about the yacht and every time we drove by the harbor I'd ask which boat was ours and if we could take a ride on it. My parents always had some excuse why we couldn't just then and, over time, I guess I stopped asking. The yacht, however, lived on in my imagination. As we made our last drive by the harbor en route to our new apartment on the north side of the city, my ten-year-old curiosity couldn't stand it any longer. "Aren't we going to take our yacht with us?" I asked. My parents thought it incredible that I still believed that story—and I couldn't believe that I had been living under a delusion all those years. In the world as children see it, all things, no matter how ridiculous or incredible, are possible, especially if your parents say so.

- Driving by the apartment where Bill and I lived after we got married, we decided to point it out to the kids. "See that orange brick building with the awnings? That's where Mommy and Daddy lived when we got married," we told them. "But where were we?" Aliza wanted to know. "You weren't born yet," we told her. "Well, where *was* I? At grandma's?" she asked. "No, silly," Benjamin said. "*I* was there and *you* were in Mommy's tummy." "Wrong," we said gently. Imagine his surprise when he found out that he wasn't there either. Both kids chewed on that revelation for a long, long time. The world as they see it, could only exist with them in it.

To be honest, it's hard to remember life before the children, let alone life *without* them. LBC (Life Before Children) is a hazy conglomeration of school, work, travel, rest (oh, yes, the picture's coming clearer now...), and crazy risk-taking that makes me shudder now. Perhaps LBC is blurry because I had only my own vision then. Now I am fortunate to have dual perspective: the world as I see it and the world as the children see it. Viewed that way, it's a more curious and wonderful place.

AREN'T THE CLOUDS BEAUTIFUL? THEY LOOK LIKE BIG BALLS OF COTTON...
PEANUTS
by SCHULZ
I COULD JUST LIE HERE ALL DAY, AND WATCH THEM DRIFT BY...
IF YOU USE YOUR IMAGINATION, YOU CAN SEE LOTS OF THINGS IN THE CLOUD FORMATIONS... WHAT DO YOU THINK YOU SEE, LINUS?
WELL, THOSE CLOUDS UP THERE LOOK TO ME LIKE THE MAP OF THE BRITISH HONDURAS ON THE CARIBBEAN..
THAT CLOUD UP THERE LOOKS A LITTLE LIKE THE PROFILE OF THOMAS EAKINS, THE FAMOUS PAINTER AND SCULPTOR...
AND THAT GROUP OF CLOUDS OVER THERE GIVES ME THE IMPRESSION OF THE STONING OF STEPHEN...I CAN SEE THE APOSTLE PAUL STANDING THERE TO ONE SIDE...
UH HUH...THAT'S VERY GOOD... WHAT DO YOU SEE IN THE CLOUDS, CHARLIE BROWN?
8-14
WELL, I WAS GOING TO SAY I SAW A DUCKY AND A HORSIE, BUT I CHANGED MY MIND!
SCHULZ

MOMMMM!
© 1986 Universal Press Syndicate
I'M THIRSTY!
WATTERSON
WHAT'S THIS? JUST WATER?
2-22

WHAT'S WRONG?
MY CAR KEYS ARE MISSING! COMPLETELY LOST!
GEE, I WONDER IF THEY REALLY ARE LOST?
DIK BROWNE
NO, THEY'RE STILL HERE
TOYS
4-15
cobean

The World As They See It

"I can't come out now — I'm taking a nap."

"Let's play pregnant. I'll shave and you'll throw up."

Bo Brown
"Want to hear my mother count to ten?"
For Better or For Worse
By Lynn Johnston
CRAAACK!
RRRUMBLE!
ISN'T THE LIGHTNING BEAUTIFUL, BUNNY?
CRACK!
AN' THUNDER IS THE ANGELS PLAYING THEIR DRUMS!
RRUMBLE
CRAAACK!
POOR ELIZABETH - I SHOULD CHECK ON HER. SHE'LL BE TERRIFIED!
CRACK!
ELIZABETH?
© 1985 Universal Press Syndicate
SCREEEEEEAM!!

The World As They See It

S. GROSS

"Good! Now we can go back to watching television."

The World As They See It

"Now run outside and play."

"Yes, ma'am, . . . I have my rubbers on."

"I hope I'm getting my own room."

"Here you go, Mom—breakfast in bed!"

"I finally persuaded Joey to eat all his spaghetti. I told him it was worms"

ROTHCO

Corka — *Today's Health*

"He's got an unfair advantage — his television set has been out of order all week."

EVERYTHING I KNOW UP TO THIS POINT IN MY LIFE...
... I HAVE LEARNED FROM TELEVISION.
I'M WHAT YOU MIGHT CALL "SESAME STREET-WISE"!
1-31
© 1986 Tribune Media Services, Inc. All Rights Reserved
BUSINO
"I'M AN ONLY CHILD— WHAT'S YOUR RACKET?"

Whiting ROTHCO
"And they bawl me out for spilling my milk!"

"You've failed, utterly!"

"Mummy! Mummy! Daddy's batteries have run out!"

"It's a single-parent family and a social worker."

"Grandma, what did you do before you had us to play with?"

"I don't know what my father does all day. All I know is it makes him sick at his stomach."

"IS IT COLD OUT TODAY ?"

"If they're going to deliver it, why do you have to go to the hospital?"

"This is my Dad's toy, once a week he comes in here and tries to pick it up."

"Use your imagination, dear. Pretend it has batteries."

"Room service!"

"Look, honey! He's standing!"

Family 3

When I was young, my father occasionally would talk about the early days of my sister's colicky life. I don't remember now what would prompt the telling, but I do remember vividly the picture he painted of one miserable night: the hot, sticky August night (and I'm sure there were many) he was so desperate to escape her screams that he stuck his head under a pillow and wrapped it around his ears in an attempt to deaden the sound.

I'm not sure what that story meant to me as a child. Perhaps it was a reminder that my sister and I hadn't changed very much over the years, because we still screamed a lot, only for different reasons. But I remembered it with a jolt one hot, sticky September night when I was walking my newborn son who was screaming with colic. Suddenly this little light went on in my brain. Parading around in my nightgown, near tears together with the crying baby, I said, "So *this* is what he was talking about!" I felt my father's exhaustion, agony, and uncertainty in a way I never had before. It connected me to his youth, connected us as parents. For that moment we were contemporaries, sharing the same miseries. And it was comforting to know that we were not alone.

The revelation I had that night marked the beginning of an entirely new perspective for me. How fascinating to see my past from my parents' vantage point, to stand together as parents. Hundred of questions occurred to me. I wanted to know how my mother coped with early parenthood. How did she get out of the house? Did she or my dad have friends with babies to share their days of confusion with? Did they use babysitters?

Over the years my questions have not ebbed, although I may not always ask them. Now that my children are old enough to choose their friends, for example, I'm not always pleased with their choices. I pause to wonder what my parents thought of my choices in friends and whether they wanted, as much as I do, to have a voice in the selection. I remember my mother's anger when a friend would treat me badly. It's the same fury that wells up in me when my children's playmates are cruel.

And I suddenly see many instances when my parents didn't interfere, like the time I was in kindergarten and didn't want to go to school because a substitute teacher wouldn't let me go to the bathroom. My mother said we would walk to school together and when I got to the door I could decide whether or not to go in. I'm sure she thought once I got there, I'd decide to go to school. Not me. I walked to school, stood at the door with the other children, and said, "No." We went home. I don't remember a lecture or anger. She let the decision be mine. I admire the strength it took to stand back and let me make my own decisions, and later, to make my own mistakes. Making these decisions is not as easy as it looks when you're a child.

Our children help us remember and relive pieces of our own childhood. Towel-drying Benjy and Aliza on the beach each summer I have a tactile and olfactory memory of my mother doing the same for me, summer after summer. I can feel the warmth of the sun as I remember sitting wrapped up on someone's lap; I can smell the mixture of suntan lotion, sand, and sweat. I know the comfort my children feel as I do the same for them. But as I remember through my children the lost bits and pieces of my childhood, I also reexamine those memories from a parent's perspective. What did my mother feel as she dried us at the beach? Was she impatient to get home? Was she enjoying the closeness?

And what about our grandparents, aunts, uncles, cousins? To think of them all as parents, of the times they were struggling to raise families, helps me to understand them better. When occasionally I think my lot in life is hard, I think about my grandparents with their three boys in their small apartment trying to make a living and a life in a new country. Or the stories my parents tell of staying up at night to keep the mice from biting my sister when she was a baby. A few cockroaches don't seem like much in comparison.

As much as being a parent has opened my eyes to the past, it compels me to imagine the future, too. I think often about the memories we are making for our children. When they are towel-drying their children on the beach (and I hope they'll have children, so they can forgive our failings), will their bodies remember how they felt too? Sometimes I imagine this chain of generations of parents and children wrapped in towels on the beach, each generation remembering its own childhood as it forms memories for its children.

When I've been a particularly cranky mom, I wonder if that's all they'll remember, or if they'll also remember the family sharing fun and games and laughter and love. When I watch the loving and lavish care Aliza heaps on her baby doll Jamie, the swaddling and kisses and bedmaking and tender caresses, I'm pretty certain the memories we are making are good ones. Already she is recreating the love of her early days. When she has her own family, this will come back to her.

Family—that collection of nutty and wonderful strangers you're related to—grows more important when you start your own family. Your relatives acquire new roles when you have children. My sister became my children's aunt. My parents became their grandparents. As much as we may treasure our own relationships with these people, how much more valuable they become now that they have special importance to your children. The delight my parents and sister take in my children is returned in at least equal measure by my kids. Their love for each other is so deep it's almost mystical, and I am thrilled by it.

My uncle, upon hearing that we are expecting another child, said to my husband and me, "I heard your good news—I mean *our* good news." This is family—this sense of continuity, of connectedness. Who else would consider the addition of each child a cause for celebration?

No. We are not going to call him Vince Lombardi Joe Montana George Patton Clint Eastwood Punch Press Teddy Roosevelt Abromowitz.

Lorenz

"Think. You're sure you haven't forgotten anything?"

Family

"Don't aim him this way!"

"It hit me all of a sudden, Joe, that I wasn't spending enough time with the children."

Family

"We're calling him 'Quits.' "

"I'll have to call you back, Marge. It's Mother's Day and I haven't got a second!"

"My father says I musn't sell more than six hundred dollars worth or he can't list me as a tax exemption."

"Hurry up, dear, your breakfast cereal's barely audible."

"We wish you every joy, dear Dad, on this your special day. . . ."

1

2

3

4

5

6

7

8

9

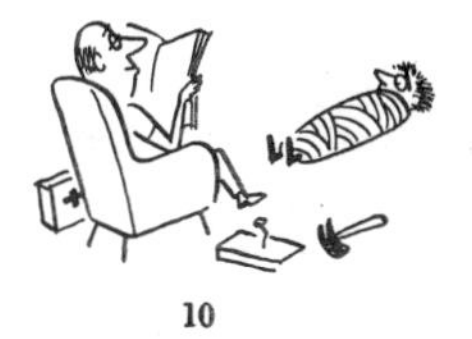

10

"Do you have anything that takes the father's side?"

BERNHARDT
INSTRUCTIONS FOR ASSEMBLY
THIS ALWAYS HAPPENS WHEN DAD IS MY BABY SITTER
HE TAKES LONGER NAPS THAN I DO!
DIK BROWNE
3-21

Family

"I never really rallied after the birth of my first child."

Growing Pains 4

They don't tell you much about what it *feels* like to be a parent before you become one. You could read yourself silly about nutrition and discipline, toilet teaching and preschool. When you're pregnant you believe that if you read all that stuff, then you'll know just what to do when you're a parent. Just like you think that if you master all the breathing techniques, you'll know just what to do during labor.

It's not that those things are useless. But how much more useful they'd be if someone talked about how you're going to feel, or at least the different range of feelings when you first confront the deep blue eyes of your newborn. Or when you're pacing the floor with your five month old for the sixth time that night. Or when your kid falls and bleeds for the first time. Or when you send her off to preschool. To me, how you feel is the heart of the matter. Because your feelings will often direct you in a way that the "ten commandments of toilet teaching" or whatever child care bible you've just read will not.

Everyone talks about your child's growing pains: stranger anxiety, separation anxiety, Oedipal and Elektra complexes, and all the cruel lessons that experience will deal him. But no one tells you that parents suffer growing pains as well, and usually along with their child. They may be about the same issues. When my children were infants I was sure that only I, or maybe a select few others, could handle them properly. So, I developed stranger anxiety myself. I didn't want anyone who hadn't had his finger prints checked with the FBI or graduated from the super-deluxe school of child rearing (which I, myself of course, had never attended) to come near my babies.

And sometimes the pains are just that, pains. Our internal wincing from the real or imagined hurts our children experience. When my son cried the day I left him at preschool (after three weeks of sitting in class with him...) I cried too. I felt his fear. And even though I knew that learning to separate was a positive step and that he would be stronger for it, I still *hurt* for him.

Of course, the lessons I learned from and through my son made me a different parent to my daughter. And she is a different child. When I left her at preschool (after staying with her for ten minutes!), she waved happily and went to climb on the jungle gym. I was pleased and proud that she separated so easily but a bit saddened too. To be sure, one of the most painful growing pains of parenting is learning to let go.

But don't get me wrong. Growing pains can also feel wonderful. There's nothing like the feeling you get when your child masters a skill, be it karate or eating without spilling half of whatever it is on the floor. The kid's proud, you're proud, all's well with the world. And when they gain more subtle, though no less crucial, skills like making friends, controlling anger, sharing, defusing an explosive situation, or laughing at themselves, the pride we feel is that much greater. I watch my children hone and polish these skills each day and I can only marvel at them. I'd like to think our children learn these skills through our example, but I think that's only partially true. It's a painful kind of growing to realize what parts of you you'd like your children to copy and which you'd rather they ignored. (I worried that my daughter's initial shyness, for example, was an inheritance from me.) Sometimes these realizations can prompt actual change in *us*, as we attempt to show our children, rather than just tell them, how we'd like them to behave.

Did you ever notice that children seem so much smarter and more clever than we could ever hope to be? They don't know that, though. At least not right away. Our children expect us to know all the right answers. "Is God dead?" Aliza asks. "How was the world created?" Benjy asks, certain that we know the answers. Little do they know the terror they strike in the hearts of us poor parents, valiantly trying to answer them honestly, forthrightly, on their level, even when we don't know the answer ourselves. And how embarrassing not to know how the TV works, for instance, or how to explain what makes a rainbow. It is part of their growing pains to discover that parents don't know everything. Sure, we may tell them that ourselves, but they don't really listen. It's not what they want to hear. They need to discover it for themselves.

Of course, once they figure it out, our children often conclude that we don't know *anything*. I still remember the shock I felt as a teenager when I discovered the rebellious acts my father had pulled while serving in World War II. Was this the same man I ate breakfast with every morning, with whom I differed so politically? Perhaps we weren't so different after all. Perhaps he knew and felt a few things I hadn't given him credit for. (And I hadn't given him credit for much during those years....)

My husband and I are beginning to see signs of the "you don't know anything" posture in our six-and-a-half year old. "Why?" "Who said?" "You can't make me." "NO!" and "I won't" are beginning to crowd out our conversations. Overnight, it seems, our sweet, pliable, eager-to-please child has turned into a vacillating pre-pre-preadolescent. This is a painful part of growing for us. Just like it was painful to learn that discipline was a friend, not a foe, and that limits, rules, manners were important weapons in the parenting arsenal. Weapons, that is, like vaccines against diseases.

I know it's painful for our son, too. After a particularly bad day between us, he'll creep back into our laps, desperate to reestablish the old intimacy. It's the same rhythm we felt when our children began to walk. Away they went, ecstatic with freedom, until panic crept in and, stumbling back to bury their heads in our laps, they returned. Escape and reunion. The pattern will be repeated over and over again throughout their lives.

Growing pains—theirs and ours. No matter how creative and patient we are, we just may not be able to affect our children's behavior all the time. Sometimes the only answer is to wait and have faith that they'll outgrow it. Hopefully, we'll live that long!

"I'd keep him home from school . . .

. . . for a few days."

"HOW CAN I TELL IF SOMETHING'S WRONG UNTIL I ***DO*** IT?"

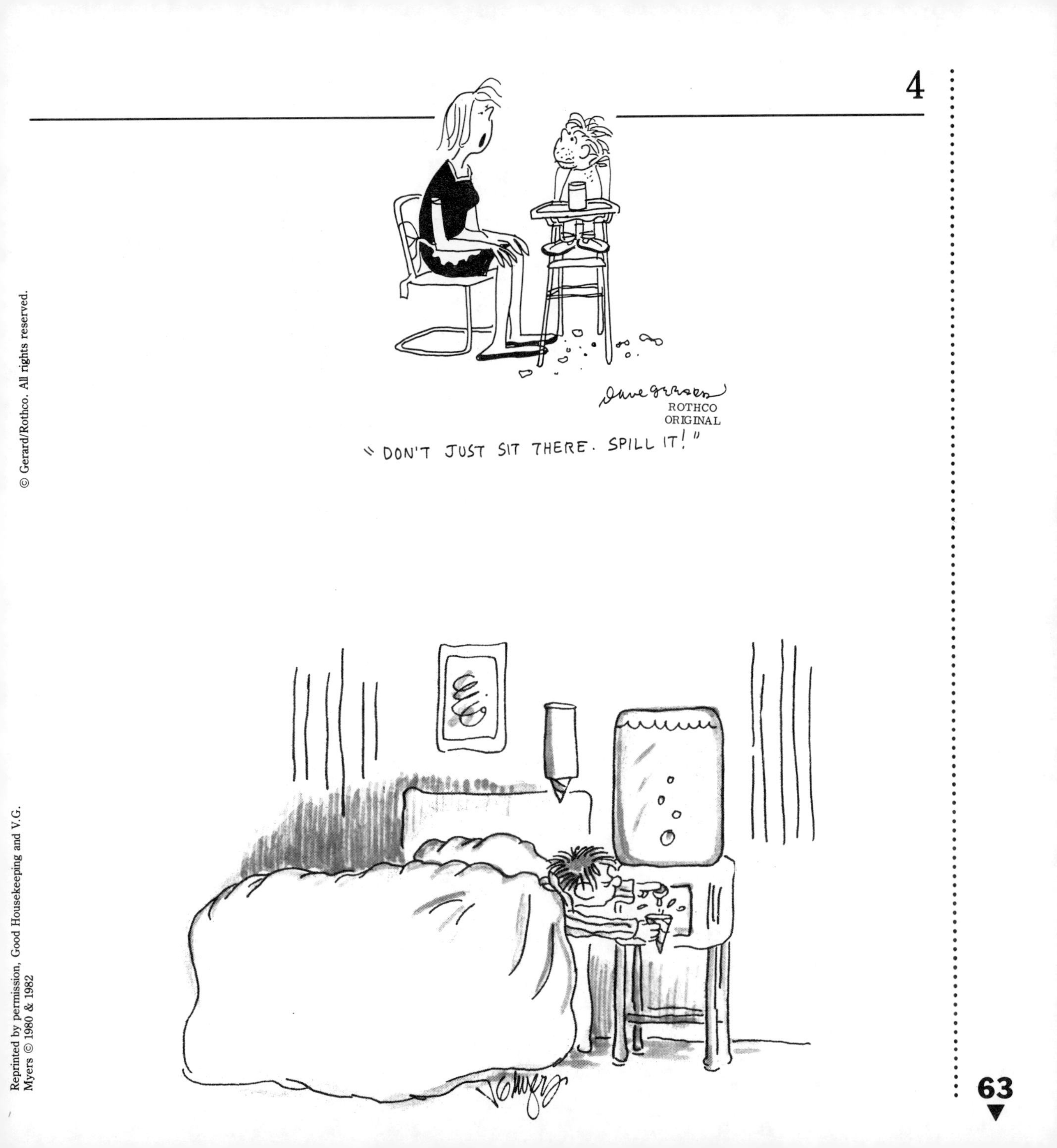

"DON'T JUST SIT THERE. SPILL IT!"

"You explain it to her."

" I get this excruciating pain when I hear the word 'Mom'."

"What are you going to be if the neighbors let you grow up?"

"BUT I JUST TOOK A BATH THIS MORNING!"

"Now look what you've done!"

1

2

3

"Time to get up, Billy—first day of school!"

LARRY
cathy
DOES LEE WANT THE BIG BALL?
NO. LEE DOESN'T WANT THE BIG BALL.
DOES LEE WANT THE FUNNY DOLL?
NO. LEE DOESN'T WANT THE FUNNY DOLL.
DOES LEE WANT THE BOOK OF FRENCH VERB CONJUGATIONS?
YES! LEE WANTS THE BOOK OF FRENCH VERB CONJUGATIONS!!
Bonjour Bébé
IS IT OKAY IF I TAKE LEE TO THE KITCHEN WITH ME, MARY ANNE?
BE MY GUEST, CATHY! IT'S SUCH A RELIEF FOR HER TO BE AROUND SOMEONE WHO ISN'T QUESTIONING MY AUTHORITY!
MY MOTHER HAS ONE SET OF RULES... MY FRIENDS WITH CHILDREN HAVE OTHER SETS OF RULES...
EVERY TIME WE VISIT ANYONE, IT TAKES A WEEK TO GET HER BACK ON TRACK.
YOU'RE THE ONE PERSON I CAN TRUST TO NOT MIX HER UP WITH YOUR OWN IDEAS OF MOTHERING!
HALLOWEEN
© 1985 Universal Press Syndicate
...JUST DON'T LET HER NEAR ANY CANDY. WE'RE RAISING HER IN A 100% SUGAR-FREE ENVIRONMENT.
LIFE AS YOU KNEW IT IS OVER, MARY ANNE.
HALLOWEEN
Guisewite 11-3

"Aw, what a gyp! I just PRETENDED I was takin' a nap and I fell asleep for REAL!"

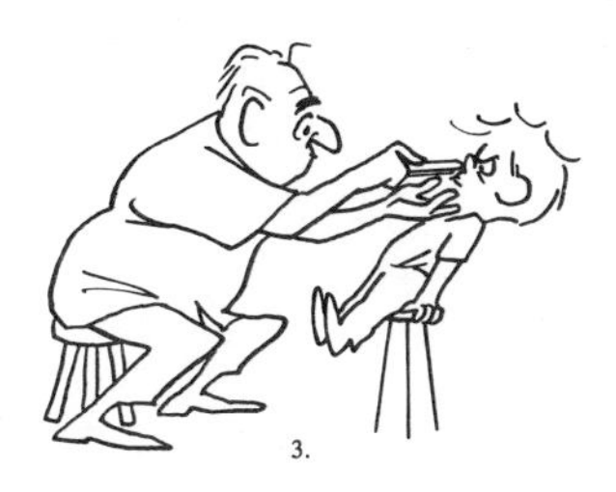

"DID YOU ASK FOR A BOY WHEN YOU GOT ME, OR DID YOU LET THE DOCTOR SURPRISE YOU?"

"IT'S TRUE. YOU WERE ACTUALLY BORN A BEAUTIFUL PRINCESS BUT YOU WERE GIVEN TO US TO BE BROUGHT UP, ... AND THERE'S NOT A DAMNED THING YOU CAN DO ABOUT IT!"

" ONE THING THEY'VE TAUGHT ME ALREADY-
$10 DOESN'T BUY MUCH . "

HERMAN
by Jim Unger
DAD.
WAH
© 1985 Universal Press Syndicate
JUST TESTING.

"Why do I keep asking questions, dad?"

"We're rather worried about William."

cathy
WHAT ARE YOU DOING THIS WEEK-END, CATHY ?
NOTHING.
...NOTHING...
IF I WERE SINGLE AND HAD A THREE-DAY WEEKEND, I'D JUST SIT AND DO NOTHING, CATHY!
THAT'S ONLY FUN FOR ABOUT 15 MINUTES, MARY ANNE.
THEN YOU START FEELING GUILTY FOR WASTING A SPECIAL WEEKEND.
BABY POWDER
YOU CALL TEN SINGLE FRIENDS AND GET TEN ANSWERING MACHINES.
YOU REALIZE THE ONLY PEOPLE WHO DIDN'T LEAVE TOWN FOR THE WEEKEND ARE YOU AND 400,000 MARRIED COUPLES.
YOU DECIDE TO WRITE LETTERS... THEN ASK, "FOR WHAT?" YOU DECIDE TO START PROJECTS... THEN THINK, "WHO CARES?"
YOU REALIZE YOU'RE TOTALLY INCAPABLE OF ENTERTAINING YOURSELF.
ALONE AND WORTHLESS, YOU SLIDE INTO A COMA OF SELF-PITY... A MISERABLE BLOB OF DEPRESSION BRIGHTENED ONLY BY THE IDEA THAT ON TUESDAY YOU GET TO GO BACK TO THE IDIOTIC JOB YOU WERE SO ANXIOUS TO HAVE A VACATION FROM!
WANT TO TRADE PLACES?
YOU MUST BE JOKING.

The Experts Say 5

Have you noticed how many experts on childrearing there are? I'm talking especially about all the doctors who have written books. You know they've been so busy with their practice and their writing that they were never home to interact with their *own* children. I'm talking about the experts who say let your three month old cry if she wakes in the middle of the night but who never themselves had the heartache of listening to a crying, hungry baby. I'm talking about all the childless women who think they know everything about raising children because they have friends with children; they feel free to give advice based on their own opinions of someone else's experience. I'm talking about grandmothers in the park and grandfathers in the grocery store, about sales clerks and librarians, just to mention a few.

I remember being overwhelmed by advice when I had my first child. Elderly neighbors, who had never been interested in me before, were suddenly invested in whether Benjamin was under- or overdressed, whether he was breast-or bottle-fed, and how often I took him outside. The continuous stream of advice only increased the feeling of ineptitude that already hugged me like a shroud. Especially when you're so new at parenting, so unsure of your own instincts and judgment, it seems incumbent upon you to weigh each opinion as if all have equal merit.

I was confident enough to pass up one piece of advice, though. One day I was riding on the elevator with our upstairs neighbor when she said to me, "You know, your son is just like an alarm clock. He wakes me up every morning at 5 o'clock." True enough, 5 A.M. was Benjy's standard wake-up time. I didn't know he disturbed our neighbor, though, and I truly felt bad. "Why don't you try drugging him?" she suggested, clearly expecting that the idea would appeal to me. (I'm surprised she didn't notice my mouth drop open at the suggestion.) As it happened, shortly after that conversation Benjy altered his sleeping pattern and woke up a little later, and a little more quietly, in the morning. As chance would have it, I again wound up in the elevator with this lady. "Well," she said brightly, "I see those drugs are working!"

Looking back I can chuckle over some of my favorite examples of advice—or perhaps it's more accurate to call them expressions of concern—from strangers when the children were babies. Now I can supply the retorts which, of course, I never had the courage to use then. For instance, when I was carrying Benjy or Aliza in the Snuggly while doing errands, someone invariably would ask me, "Are you sure the baby can breathe in there?" (This would be said with the clear intimation that the kid could not breathe.) "No," my instant response should've been. "I'm committing public infanticide by suffocation and you came along just in time." Or, when out for a stroll on a warm spring day, someone would always ask me (usually while waiting for the traffic light to change), "Do you think the baby's warm enough?" (This, too, would be said with an accusing intonation.) I should've said, "Yes, the beads of sweat indicate that she's quite comfortable." And, of course, there was always someone around to suggest that Aliza would get some disease from her pacifier or else choke on her bagel.

But where, where, where are these experts now? I'd like them to tell me so many things—like how to keep two children happy and solve their squabbles without yelling, like how to make sure both kids are treated equally by everyone, like how to guide them into independence without losing your mind, like how to find appropriate punishments for all the different misbehaviors, like how to instill in them self-esteem, patience, inner drive, moral values.

Now that my children are almost five and seven, no one's coming up to me on the street anymore. Babies, it seems, require interference that older children don't. Now that the problems are more complex, where are all those experts? Why is it that most books concentrate only on younger children? Probably because it's easier to talk about the early push for independence in the terrible twos than it is to discuss it in the later years. No one seems to care whether my kids are dressed warmly enough these days. I guess they figure that if I got them this far, I can do the rest on my own without botching it up too badly.

But now is when I really need someone's expert help. And where do I turn? To the real experts – to moms and dads who are struggling with similar issues, experimenting with various coping techniques and seeing what works (and mostly what doesn't!). These real experts don't have pat solutions; they have ideas and suggestions. Try this, try that, this helped me, maybe it will help you.

I know I'll get a sympathetic ear when I call a friend who has children because my own are driving me crazy or because one of them is behaving in a way that worries me. I know other parents will take my worries seriously while still giving me a perspective which will alleviate many of my fears. Often these terrible things we keep secret and then share (like our kids learning four-letter words) turn out to be things other kids are doing too. With these parents I can let my hair down and talk about the screaming, impatient, never-good-enough parent I feel I am. They never see me that way. And their perspective is a welcome relief, a relief that all the advice in the world could not replace.

When the children were babies and I cried to my parents about the sleepless nights, the feeding battles, the tantrums and the illnesses, they would cluck sympathetically. Then my father, with a wisdom I could not then comprehend, would say to me, "Little kids, little problems; big kids, big problems." At the time I could not imagine what could be bigger problems than the ones I had. I've learned, of course, that he was right. Problems like scheduling my whole life around naps, learning how to (and remembering to) distract rather than say no, racing for a bathroom in the grocery store during those first days without diapers, do not seem as earth-shattering as the new problems I'm confronting. Problems like lying, not doing homework, sexual exploration. I'm sure that, as my father suggested, with each new age I'll look back with nostalgia at the problems I've conquered, or at least at those the children have outgrown. And I'll be grateful for those comforting words of advice that other parents have graciously offered.

The Experts Say

"I've checked again...there isn't a war toy in the lot."

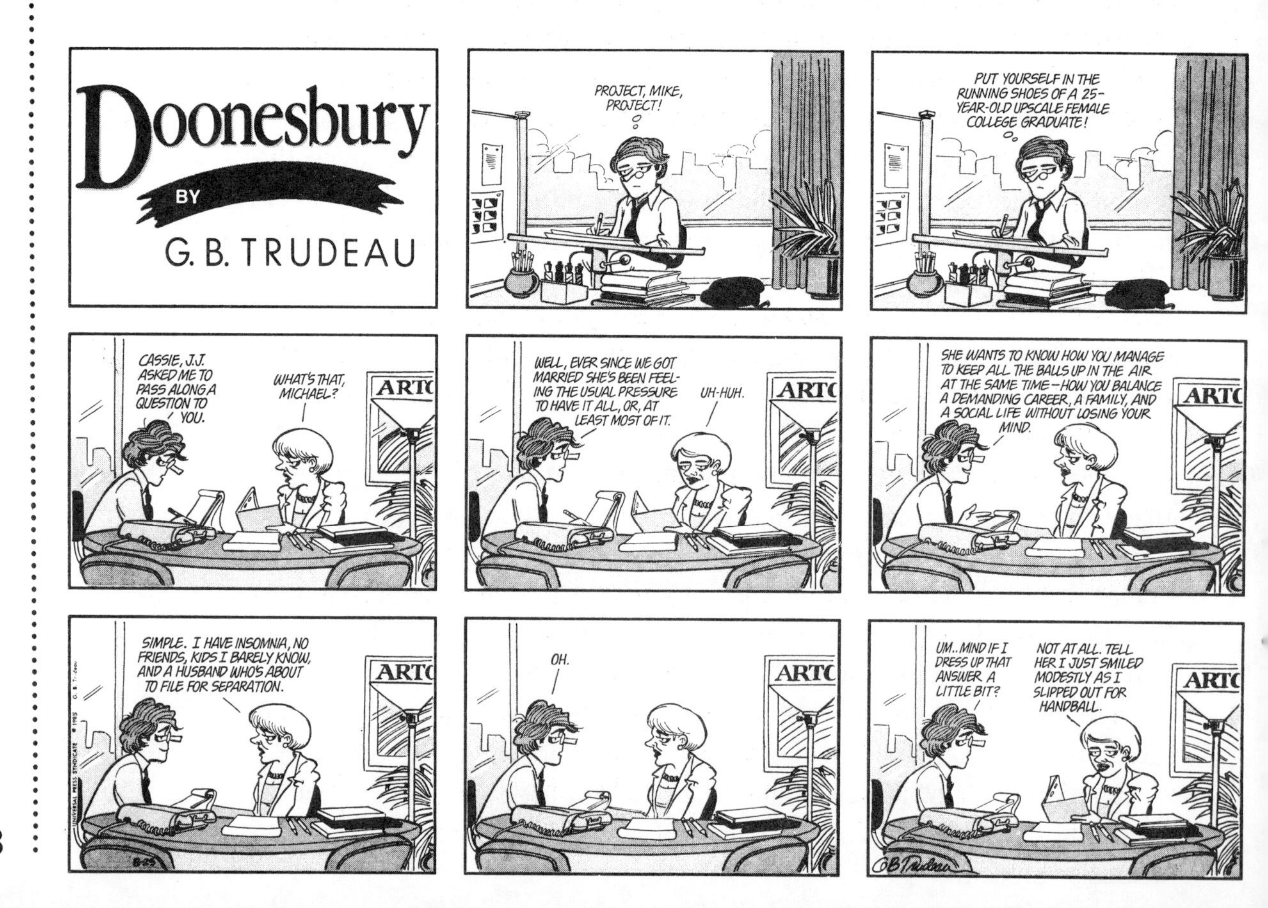

"Letting each child have his own pets enhances his sense of individuality and helps develop a sense of responsibility."

The Experts Say

Saturday Evening Post

"I still say you're spoiling him!"

"Parents can ease sibling tension by encouraging each child to have his own friends."

CHILD PSYCHIATRIST
CHILD PSYCHIATRIST
Filchock
cathy
I'M GLAD YOU COULD COME OVER, CATHY.
HOOCHEY COOCHEY EEKY BEEKY BOOKEY BOO
IT'S SO REFRESHING TO HEAR SOME ADULT CONVERSATION FOR A CHANGE.
DIAPERS... STROLLER... POWDER... BLANKET... FRESH CLOTHES... TISSUES... BABY WIPES... BAGGIES... PINS... BIBS... BONNETS... RATTLES...
WE'RE ONLY GOING TO BE GONE FOR 45 MINUTES, MARCIA.
BUNNY BOOK...DOGGY BOOK...CLOWN BOOK... TEDDY BEAR...DOLLS... MUSIC BOX...
45 MINUTES, MARCIA.
BUSY BOX... CRAYONS... BALLS... BLOCKS... MOBILES...
MARCIA, IN ONE MONTH YOU'VE GONE FROM BEING A FUN FRIEND TO A TRAVELING BABY BOUTIQUE!!!
KIM'S RESTAURANT
WAAAH!
DIDN'T YOU BRING ANYTHING ELSE?
Guisewite 8-5

"Would you have a moment, dear, to share Ivy's dissatisfaction?"

"Of course, his father was very musical."

"Stop worrying about him, he'll get bald as he gets older."

"I understand you are a gifted child. I was a gifted child myself."

THEY SAY IT'S NORMAL FOR A THREE-YEAR-OLD TO BE AFRAID OF THUNDER
GEE, TRIXIE IS VERY ADVANCED
SHE ISN'T ONE YET AND ALREADY SHE'S SCARED TO DEATH
3-24
DIK BROWNE
© 1986 King Features Syndicate, Inc. World rights reserved.
CHILD PSYCHOLOGY
Mervyn Wilson

Why Did We Have Children? 6

There are certain moments, and I'm sure all of us can remember several without even pausing, when we've questioned the sanity of our decision to have children. Right now, for instance, I'm picturing the faces around last night's dinner table. There was Benjamin. Asked to please not shovel huge quantities of food into his mouth at once and to chew with his mouth closed, he responded immediately by spooning an immense helping of casserole into his mouth and, after only a single chew, treating us to an open-mouthed view of the carnage. Giggling at my disapproval, some of the food, of course, cascaded out of his mouth and onto the plate, among other things.

Then there was Aliza, who is perhaps the slowest eater in the history of western civilization, but who can be prompted to consume large quantities quickly by—you guessed it—her brother's shoveling of food in and showing it off soon thereafter. This was so hilarious, she thought, that she proceeded, together with Benjamin, to gobble large portions of casserole, open her mouth to show me, let some dribble out, then swallow the rest. Between gobbling and giggling she could barely breathe.

This, in turn, was followed by abortive attempts on my part at conversation with my husband. The script went something like this: "So, Bill, did you" "Mom can we" "Just a minute, I was asking daddy a ques" "But I just want to" "I said you'll have to wait" "AAAAAWWW" "Okay, okay what's your question?" "Can we watch TV?" "No, now let me ask Daddy" "But why not?" "Because" "Ow, he kicked me" "I did not" "Moooom"...ad infinitum. (But direct a question *to* a child—"Honey, what did you do in art class today?" for instance—and you're lucky if you get so much as a grunt.)

Are *your* children selectively deaf? Mine are. Their ears seem unable to receive messages along the frequency of my voice, or their father's. I can be face to face with my daughter, talking to her, and still get a blank, vacant stare. Interestingly enough, though, this same child can, at a range of two thousand feet or more, hear me whisper to my husband that we might have ice cream for dessert.

Do your children want you *only* when you've just made a telephone call? I usually wait to make a call until they are off someplace playing, or until they've been taken upstairs to get ready for bed. But, being children, they are resistant to the idea that I need contact with the outside world. I don't know how they know I'm on the phone. Perhaps it's a sixth sense that children have and outgrow by the time they reach adulthood. All I know is that as soon as someone answers at the other end, children materialize at my elbow crying, fighting, or demanding some assistance. My phone calls are a longer version of my earlier conversation with my husband. Only these are more likely to include threats and ultimatums.

Speaking of sixth senses, there's another I recall. When Aliza was a baby and stayed up half the night crying, it never disturbed Benjamin. I always marvelled at his ability to sleep through her high-pitched shrieks. When she had calmed down and I was sure she was asleep, I'd tiptoe back to bed. It never failed that, just as the covers were pulled up and my mind was blessedly blank, either Benjamin would be at my side or I'd hear him calling me from the next room. Out of bed I'd trot. I remember thinking, "How can he sense that I'm available? If only he'd get me on the way back to bed, I could tolerate it better." But once I was back under the covers, it was torture to get out of bed again. Those were moments I questioned why I ever wanted children in the first place.

The exasperations of parenthood include things like: children wanting food only after all food has been removed from the table and all the dishes have been put away; children needing to go to the bathroom as soon as you've left the one store that has a restroom (and of course you asked if she had to go *before* you left); brothers only wanting a certain toy when sisters are using it, and vice versa; apple juice being spilled on the floor only after you've just mopped it; children getting sick when an important event, holiday, or trip is planned. And the list goes on and on.

But I don't think it's the exasperating moments that challenge our desire for children. After all, as frustrating as some of those things are, they're pretty funny, too. I think the times we really wonder why we had children have more to do with our feelings of powerlessness and of never quite knowing the right thing to do at the right time.

I remember Benjy's first year, when every time we traveled, be it by car or plane, we carried with us a ton of diapers as well as several changes of clothes. We never used all the things we brought, and especially on planes we found it difficult to carry everything. So, on one flight home from visiting the grandparents in Florida, we decided to keep it reasonable: three diapers and one change of clothes. That's all. Shortly after we boarded the plane, Benjamin became ill with some sort of stomach flu. He proceeded to have diarrhea regularly throughout the two-hour flight. By the time we reached New York, we had gone through all our diapers and clothes (as well as worn out our welcome on the plane!). You could say we guessed wrong. Parents, the old saying goes, are never right.

We laughed that situation off, but the feeling remained that no matter what choices we make, with whatever information or experience, somewhere along the line our lack of foresight or lack of insight will be revealed to us. There are times when I've punished the children for some conduct and then realized how wrong I was, and other times when I haven't punished them and felt that leniency, too, was not right. There have been times when I've tried to be sensitive to a child and helped him to talk about something when all he really wanted was to be left alone, and other times when I've honored his seeming desire for privacy and discovered it was just a sham. At times I hung on tight to their babyhood when they needed room to be independent; other times when they needed to be babied I pushed them to stand on their own two feet. There have been times when I accused one child of doing something when actually it was the other, and times when I yelled a lot for days, not because the kids were behaving worse than usual, but because I was frustrated about something that had nothing to do with them. And then there've been times when I don't yell at all because I feel guilty for the times I yelled for no reason. Or simply because I don't have the energy.

The moments when, deep down, I say, "Why *did* we have children?" have little to do with the transitory moments of rage, aggravation, and exhaustion. Instead, they are the result of the knowledge that what we have is so precious and of the nagging sense that we are not always worthy of the gift.

"Why, Mrs. Johnson, I hoped you were going to bring your little boy with you again."

" PROMISE NOT TO GET MAD IF I TELL YOU SOMETHING I HAVE TO DO."

David Langdon "Like I always say, it depends on the way you bring children up." Copr. © 1968 David Langdon

Why Did We Have Children?

American Le

"I have to go to the bathroom."

Garel

"They were no trouble at all. I let them run around till they got good and tired."

"Let me know just before you reach the limit of your patience, will you, Ma?"

"LOOKING FOR ME ?"

GUESS WHO'S OUR NEW DEN MOTHER ?

Why Did We Have Children?

Fine/Good Housekeeping

"'Up' is pretty darn' high. Because they flap their wings to make them fly. It's wet for the same reason that anything without water is dry. Sunday just happens to follow Saturday, that's all. And he couldn't tell a lie because his father saw him cut the tree down. Now, do you think that will hold you till bedtime?"

"Go ahead, tell me what a hard day you had at the office. . . . I dare you!"

"What's the matter with you?"

Katzman Saturday Evening Post

"It can easily be assembled by any eight-year-old with an engineering degree."

"Don't be alarmed—his aim is terrible"

"Then there are 15,000 third prizes of either a lifetime flashlight, a pocket pencil sharpener, or a six-way jackknife. Fourth prize is either a gold-dipped key chain, a vegetable knife, or . . ."

GAMES FOR NORMAL CHILDREN
FOR CHILDREN WITH ABOVE NORMAL INTELLIGENCE
ISN'T THAT CUTE?
GOO GOO GA-DA DO
MARVIN'S PRETENDING HE'S TALKING ON THE PHONE LIKE MOMMY AND DADDY
TOM ARMSTRONG

"And what does he intend to specialize in?"

Cartoon Features Syndicate

Why Did We Have Children?

"Is it okay if I get out of the tub now?"
IF I'M NOT CRYING... I'M SLEEPING...
AND IF I'M NOT SLEEPING, I'M EATING...
AND IF I'M NOT EATING, I'M SUCKING MY THUMB!
MAKES YOU WONDER WHAT PARENTS SEE IN US?
3-12

"HERE'S TO THE BEST DADDY IN THE WHOLE WORLD!"

Anderson/Saturday Evening Post

Saturday Evening Post

"Guess what it's doing out!"

6-22
© 1985 Universal Press Syndicate

NEED A HUG, DADDY?

LET'S SURPRISE YOUR PAW, TATER -- SAY "DA-DA"
GLUB GLUB
THAT'S NOT HIS NAME, HONEY-POT -- THAT'S WHAT HE DOES WITH HIS JUG
GLUB GLUB
SAY "QUACK QUACK," TATER
GLUB GLUB
SAY "MOO MOO"
GLUB GLUB
SAY "BOWSY WOWSY"
GLUB GLUB
SAY "TEDDY WEDDY"
GLUB GLUB
FRED LASSWELL
SAY "GLUB GLUB"
GLUB GLUB
PAW -- LISSEN TO TATER SAY "GLUB GLUB"
QUACK QUACK
4-13
©1986 King Features Syndicate, Inc. World rights reserved.

Why Did We Have Children?

AGE 1

AGE 2

AGE 3

AGE 4

AGE 5

AGE 6

GOOD MORNING

"In the middle of My sleep—BANG!
I hear jelly fall on a cracker."

"*You* have *to go to bed, Mommy's tired!*"

"I just wanted to kiss you."

ABOUT LEAH YARROW:

A former associate editor and frequent contributor to *Parents Magazine*, Leah Yarrow is the author of *Parents* ™ *Book of Pregnancy and Birth* (Ballantine 1984). She lives in Chicago with her husband and two children, and is currently awaiting the birth of her third child.